DON'T START FROM HERE

We Need A Banking Revolution

DAVID SHIRREFF

BOOKS

Don't Start from Here ... We Need a Banking Revolution
By David Shirreff

Half-tone cartoons by James McLean
Line cartoons by Jack Coltman

Text and illustrations © David Shirreff 2014

Published in 2014 by Crunch Books, London
www.crunchbooks.org

Crunch Books is an imprint of Arabian Publishing Ltd,
4 Bloomsbury Place, London WC1A 2QA
www.oxbowbooks.com/oxbow/arabianpublishing

Edited by William Facey

A CIP record for this book is available from the British Library

ISBN: 978-0-9929808-0-1

Typeset in Bembo and Frutiger

Typesetting and digital artwork by Jamie Crocker, Artista-Design, UK
Printed and bound by TJ International, Cornwall, UK

When the capital development of a country
becomes a by-product of the activities of a casino,
the job is likely to be ill-done

John Maynard Keynes (1883–1946)
The General Theory of Employment, Interest and Money (1936)

CONTENTS

Acknowledgements

The ideas in this book were first presented as a discussion paper at a round-table organised by the Centre for the Study of Financial Innovation (CSFI). My thanks to Andrew Hilton, director of the CSFI, for the air time and some helpful editing. Thanks also to Gary Mead at the New City Initiative and David Green at Civitas for their encouragement, as well as to the many friends, especially Will Facey at Arabian Publishing, who urged me to publish my thoughts in book form.

INTRODUCTION

The need for more radical reform

This is a call for revolution – a revolution to reduce complexity in global banks, to split them into manageable chunks, and to change the self-serving nature of the culture that dominates them.

These recommendations are not plucked out of the blue. They represent a reasonable course of action, given the mess that finance got itself into over the past two decades. Most of the remedies that I offer have already been hinted at, sporadically, by many commentators – in the letters and op-ed columns, especially of the *Financial Times*, by economists and laymen – but without being fashioned into a coherent plan. Financial-sector and banking reform has lost its way. But, in my opinion, it seems to be stumbling, half-blind, towards the solutions you find here. This is an attempt to speed up that process.

For many, the measures that I am proposing might appear too radical. But I would argue that fear of being radical has led to the situation we are in today: instead of the banking and financial sector being reformed to serve the real economy, much of the value added by the 'real' economy is still being hoovered up by the banking system. This is happening under the guise of recapitalising and strengthening bank balance sheets; in effect, however, all it is doing is sustaining a sector that is still failing to serve the real economy efficiently.

**DO NOT
GO TO JAIL**

**COLLECT £200
AS YOU PASS
GO**

PART 1

REVOLUTION

1

The Need for a New Model

The evidence that I lay out in Part 2 of this book has led me to a single, clear conclusion: we need a new model of banking (and to an extent a reworking of the entire financial system), so that it is less likely to need rescue by the taxpayer and is more likely to serve the real economy, not a narrow interest group.[1]

It is understandable that, in the present economic climate, governments are reluctant to do more than tinker with the system for fear of incurring further costs – and the further wrath of the taxpayer.

However, this is a blinkered, short-term view. We owe it to future generations to get it right, or more right, this time. As, to be fair, we did once before: the Glass-Steagall Act of 1933 was America's answer to the near-failure of the financial system. If Glass-Steagall had been kept in place, it can be

---

1 Some British regulators have made noises about the same thing, without exactly calling for a revolution. Adair Turner, as chairman of the Financial Services Authority, termed some activities of investment banks "socially useless", triggering a wide debate. Andy Haldane, executive director of the Bank of England, in a speech in October 2012, called for a "financial reformation" to tackle the approach to culture, capital and compensation. http://www.bankofengland.co.uk/publications/Documents/speeches/2012/speech616.pdf

argued that the world would not have got into such a mess in 2007/08. A new banking/financial regime is desirable.

Can we design one that won't in turn be unpicked by future generations? I think we can.

But I also think it requires a major intellectual leap in how we think about banking.

Utility principle

First of all, maybe we should think of the financial system as a utility, in the same way that we think of sewerage systems and electricity distribution. After all, the basic functions of finance are to facilitate payments and keep track of cash balances. It is not very glamorous – though, in addition, banks must safeguard deposits, pay them back on demand or on maturity, and make credit judgments on borrowers.

To inspire confidence, banks have tended to be housed in prestigious buildings. That has come to obfuscate their basic function and has given bankers an exaggerated sense of their own importance. Victorian sewage works and pumping stations were also housed in prestigious buildings, but there was no illusion about the stuff they were pumping. When it comes to banks, there is. Part of the confusion that has arisen (both in bankers' sense of their own importance and in the eyes of the broader society) comes from the contrast between the basic functions of banking and the considerable power that some bankers have wielded in the past, from financing wars to bailing out countries. That said, the recent financial crisis has shown, more strongly than in previous crises, that banking activity can readily impose a cost on society – and that this cost is not taken into account when rewards are distributed among banks' investors and employees.

Let's try to break down what exactly banks and bankers *do*.

Basic retail banking

The building-blocks of a financial system, as I understand it, are banks, a central bank, and a set of rules that govern how they should operate. Key to that is the retail bank.

First and foremost, ordinary men and women (who can also be seen as voters and taxpayers) need a reliable place to keep their cash. A bank is generally more reliable than the underside of a mattress. To maintain confidence in that bank, it must be governed by soundness principles and conduct-of-business rules. Experience also shows that retail deposits are 'stickiest' if there is some kind of deposit insurance, either from the government or from a deposit-insurance fund, or preferably both. Further soundness is secured if limits are set on how those bank deposits are used.

Even though there are always limits on what a bank can do with your money, that point is worth pressing further. For instance, a 'narrow bank' (in the sense suggested by Prof. John Kay[2]), the soundest bank thinkable, would be allowed to invest *only* in domestic government bonds of short-term maturity. Deposits at a 'narrow bank' could conceivably have an explicit 100% government guarantee. Such a bank would indeed be sound – but it might be *too* sound.[3] Rather than gaining a meagre return on government bonds, a proportion

---

2 See John Kay: Narrow Banking, published by the CSFI in 2009, and his further discussion in The Future of Finance, The LSE Report, 2010, chapter 8.

3 A few respected economists argue that a banking union across the euro zone can best be reached by re-introducing the notion of retail deposits that are 100% insured with reserves at the central bank – ie backed by risk-free central bank money. It is only in this way, they say, that deposit insurance will work regardless of which country the bank is registered in. Effectively, it would eliminate political influence on bank behaviour.

This might make sense – provided that the 100% reserves cover only the insured deposits. Other bank deposits, which would not be backed in this way, would pay a competitive rate of interest – and would be used to finance lending and the economy in general. Depositors would be aware that these deposits are at risk, but would be rewarded with higher interest rates. http://www.ceps.be/book/copernican-turn-banking-union-urgently-needed

of the deposits might prudently be put to work. Experience has shown that banks can reasonably extend their investments to (modest) mortgage lending and personal and small-company loans – at least, up to a strictly limited proportion of deposits.

In all cases, any bank, no matter how narrow, would need a level of capital to tide it over periods where late payment or losses on loans exceed the net inflow of deposits and loan service payments.

In the end, retail banks must be so robust that their failure is near-impossible. Deposit insurance – implicitly or explicitly backed by the government – means that a run on a retail bank is unlikely, unless the government itself faces bankruptcy. (Ireland, Iceland, Greece, and Cyprus have shown that this is a distinct possibility; however this is not a banking problem, but a problem of state solvency.) Because even conservatively managed retail banks tend to be allowed to make home loans and to take liens on property as security on small-business loans, they are inevitably exposed to housing and commercial property busts. But, in the eyes of the broader society, that is generally considered an acceptable and manageable risk, provided regulators insist on low loan-to-value ratios.

To be absolutely clear: *retail banks are not meant to be completely bomb-proof.* A simple retail bank does not *need* to be bomb-proof if it is a financial institution that the government cares about and would support in a crisis. But this would be the *only* kind of bank that would have such implicit or explicit support.[4]

---

4 Wiseacres will say it was retail banks, such as HBOS and Northern Rock, that got into most trouble during the crisis. The fact is, these were not simple retail banks; they were heavily interconnected with other financial players, and they had contingent lines of credit to supposedly remote strategic investment vehicles (SIVs) which they had to honour in the face of a liquidity crisis. Regulators should never have allowed them to extend themselves in that way. In April 2007, the FSA actually advised Northern Rock that it was under-using its capital and could afford to expand its business.

Who would invest in such retail banks? A deposit-taking bank that makes a modest amount of mortgage and retail loans, and invests the balance in government bonds, is unlikely to make a heady return on investment. So it would attract only the most conservative investors. A return on equity of more than 6% is unlikely. The government might even have to subsidise the business to make it attract any investors at all. But it would be safe. On balance, that would be in the long-term interest of customers and taxpayers. *In extremis* one could view this kind of banking as just another public utility, part of the necessary infrastructure – which would not rule out state or municipal ownership.

The trick would be to keep retail banks, if they are state- or municipally owned, out of the hands of politicians. The experience of the German Sparkassen (municipally owned retail banks) is that they can be very useful for supporting local businesses. But they are also in danger of being steered towards supporting prestige projects and other vote-catching schemes by local politicians and other board members.[5] That's a big problem – but it is not insuperable.

Corporate and wholesale banking

Bigger companies also need a bank which can handle complex cashflows, provide them with foreign-exchange and other services, pre-finance projects, offer buyer credits to their customers and support them through mergers, disposals and acquisitions. They also need advisers to take them through the issuing of new shares or bonds, and perhaps to

---

5 Andrew Hilton of the CSFI has proposed a banking industry modelled on the travel agency business, which is characterised by "cut-throat competition; enormous platform flexibility; very low entry/exit barriers; minimal regulation (essentially, only conduct of business/anti-fraud regulation) and virtually no day-to-day supervision; most importantly, private (or industry mutual) insurance which protects clients from the problems of the industry."

provide commodity hedges and other derivatives.

The question is: Are these services best provided by a one-stop commercial-cum-investment bank? Or should there be a clear distinction between commercial/wholesale banking and what we know as investment banking?

And, whatever the answer to that, are there dangers in allowing a single bank to provide such services? For instance, are there unmanageable conflicts of interest? And is a bank which sees all these flows likely to front-run its clients?

In my opinion, a sensible division of labour would be for the commercial/wholesale bank to provide customers with lending, cash management and standard foreign-exchange and interest-rate hedging services, but to outsource anything more complex to an investment bank. It could also provide financial support to investment banks – but only to a limited extent, and with appropriate credit and performance-risk controls so that the interconnectedness that made the collapse of Lehman Brothers so traumatic is avoided. Commercial/wholesale banks should not be allowed to make their balance sheets available for investment banks, or other shadow banks as a place to 'park' underwriting positions and other trading exposures.

I concede that a commercial/wholesale bank would need to be a critical size to achieve economies of scale. But those economies of scale must not involve cross-subsidy from a retail operation.[6] Nor should the commercial/wholesale

---

6 There is always an exception. Many have pointed to Sweden's Handelsbanken as a model retail bank which also deals with corporate customers. Handelsbanken is well worth a study as an example of a bank, active in Britain, which has limited itself to the clients and businesses that it understands, and which has a bonus system which pays out only at retirement and treats chief executive and doorman as equals (apart, reportedly, from a handful of vital investment bankers). Cross-subsidy from the retail operation does not appear to be an issue while its corporate bank is so conservative and profitable. The Handelsbanken model is impressive, but it is very selective, so could probably not be replicated nationally to provide inclusive retail and corporate banking.

bank be integrated with an investment bank to produce a 'flow monster' which, along with other similar beasts, could control pricing in the market.[7]

It is inevitable that corporate/wholesale banks that are not cross-subsidised by retail deposits will be more costly to run. Corporate financial services may therefore be more expensive. But that will reflect the real cost of doing business. If governments decide that they need to subsidise the development of certain business sectors, they can do that with loan schemes, tax breaks, or even via development funds, or perhaps a development bank – all of which would be more transparent than the current system of hidden subsidies.

Inevitably, there will be a distinction between financial services provided to less sophisticated fund managers or private investors, and those provided to investors qualified as professional counterparties.

In a simple division of labour, corporate/wholesale banks would provide basic financial services, such as cash management, custody, and foreign exchange, direct to investment clients. They would outsource more sophisticated services, such as the buying and selling of securities, derivatives and other hedging instruments to brokers or investment banks, acting as agent only – provided the client

---

7 Universal banks, such as JPMorgan Chase, Barclays and Deutsche Bank not only provide these one-stop-shop services to corporate clients. They also take retail deposits; and they have clients on the investment side which buy the securities that they issue for corporations. The retail deposits offer these universal banks a stability, and access to cheap money, that they would not otherwise enjoy. But for the retail depositor there is no obvious benefit in putting his deposits at risk with a bank that lends to big companies and deals in world markets. The depositor has no chance of sharing in the upside if the bank makes egregious profits. But he, or the taxpayer/deposit insurer, has a risk that the bank makes egregious losses. No-one testifying to the Vickers Commission or the Liikanen group of high-level experts was able to volunteer a good reason why retail customers might benefit from putting deposits with a corporate and investment bank. It is only universal bankers themselves who talk of the stability that these deposits offer the bank (because they cross-subsidise other parts of their business).

is sufficiently sophisticated and its articles of association allow it to use such instruments.[8]

Sophisticated investors might thus use corporate/wholesale banks as custodians and to provide simple financial services, but for more sophisticated trades they would need to use a broker, or an investment bank.

'Pure' merchant and investment banking

A partnership is generally reckoned to be the best model for a merchant or investment bank. In it, the partners put their own capital at risk. That makes sense. An investment bank provides advice and transaction services to clients, underwriting – if only briefly – the placing of shares or bonds, and taking equity or lending stakes to launch new ventures or reshape existing ones. The partners share unlimited personal liability for net losses sustained by the partnership.

I advocate a return of investment banking to the partnership model.

This is not simply to put the clock back to an alleged 'golden age' of investment banking; it is because there is a better alignment of interests between partners and the bank. Partners are also less likely to give employees incentives to trade recklessly, given their interest in the fortunes, good or bad, of the bank of which they are owners.[9]

---

8 In the EU various pieces of legislation attempt to provide more transparency for this kind of dealing. MiFID (the Markets in Financial Instruments Directive) requires evidence from dealers that they have found the best possible price for the client (unless the client qualifies as a sophisticated professional counterparty). But these rules are enormously cumbersome – an example of regulators trying to deal with market complexity by adding red tape.

9 Supporters of the universal banking model will say that only universal banks – one-stop-shops – can offer full banking services to the world's biggest corporations. But there is a counter-argument: these big corporations already buy services from more than one financial institution. For the really big deals they usually hire a consortium of banks and/or investment banks. They do not, and should not, use banks as one-stop-shops.

Whose capital?

Equity investors in private listed companies expect a return, either through a dividend or through capital growth. When that company is heavily regulated – as in the case of a water utility or a bank – investor expectations are slightly different. Heavy regulation *normally* means the company is likely to have steadier, but lower, profits.

Recently, investors in banks have sought consistently high returns – but have instead got more volatile returns, anything from 25% to a negative return on equity (ROE). A more stable financial sector would attract the utility-type investor, but not the chaser of high risk/high return. Can a reformed and stable financial sector offer investors attractive enough returns? Probably not, unless investors sharply lower their expectations.

Recent share issues by banks such as Deutsche Bank and Barclays have suggested a cost of capital for major international banks of around 10%. Issues of CoCos (contingent convertible bonds – subordinated debt that flips into equity if the bank performs badly) have suggested a cost of capital of around 7.5–9%, although some CoCos with a more bond-like structure have coupons closer to 5%.

This means that a Deutsche, Barclays, Credit Suisse or BNP Paribas would have to aim for a return on equity of 15% or more: these days, they are lucky if they produce a 5% return.

Given the heavy regulatory and compliance burdens that are placed on institutions categorised as systemically important, it is a huge challenge for banks to produce an ROE consistently over 10%. The risk is that the bank's executives will 'massage' returns rather than concentrate on the bank's stability and on improving service to customers.

Some adjustment of investors' expectations is therefore necessary. But it is worth emphasising that investors might also benefit from two positive effects. Simplifying banks (and banking rules) would

- reduce operating costs and the cost of compliance and regulation;
- and, in the longer run, reduce the cost of financial services to both borrowers and investors.

2

HOW TO GET THERE FROM HERE: 10 REMEDIES

This is the tricky bit …

Even those who concede that the current system is in many ways dysfunctional, are inclined to give up. We are where we are, and it would be utopian to believe in radical change. Maybe, maybe not.

Certainly, the direction of banking reform since the 2008 crisis has not inspired confidence. It is not leading to the new banking world outlined above; nor has it offered coherent answers to the shortcomings that were exposed in the years 2007 to 2010. There are two glaring failures:

- the failure to simplify the complexity; and
- the failure to change the culture that permeates the world of finance.

The big banks that dominate world finance today are still too big and too complex. Proposals to break them into smaller, more manageable pieces have been resisted tooth and nail by politicians and bankers alike – and even by regulators, either because of 'capture' or because they, too, are scared of radical change. The culture of entitlement by bankers to a disproportionate share of the financial spoils persists at regulated banks, even at those owned by thousands of small shareholders, or even by the state.

A new and tougher approach is needed. Big banks *must* be broken up – and that means not just into a 'good' bank and a 'bad' bank, as has been suggested for Royal Bank of Scotland. Functions which lead inevitably to conflicts of interest and to client abuse must be separated. Opaque cross-subsidy must end. So must oligopolistic behaviour by institutions and groups of people within institutions.

How to do it?

1. Simplify the rules ...

Most social activities need rules. Rulemakers usually strive to keep them to a minimum to keep things simple for participants and enforcers. But regulation of financial services has, in recent years, been a race to complexity: the more complex the services offered, the more regulators have attempted to capture that complexity in their rules.[10]

This must stop. It is time to go back to first principles and ask: What are the simplest rules that financial markets and institutions need in order to function? If certain financial instruments and practices don't fit inside the simplified rulebook because they are too complex to describe, then they should be exiled to the part of the market that is 'unregulated'.[11] (It should cheer the liberal-minded that, in

---

10 Take the Markets in Financial Instruments Directive (MiFID), which strives to increase the transparency of trading in equities and other instruments. It saddled dealers with a huge amount of extra reporting obligations but on deals already executed in the heat of battle. First, it does not help their customers directly to achieve a better price; second, it skews the market by demanding 'proof' that the execution price was the 'best' available.

11 This is already happening to some extent, since banks have been encouraged (by Basel

my new world, the territory occupied by investment banks, hedge funds and the like will be less hamstrung by regulation than before, on the principle of *caveat emptor*.)

2. Scrap Basel 2 and 3 ...

The Basel Committee on Banking Supervision took a wrong turning in the 1990s, and began to collude with the way that bankers themselves want to run their banks. Sound banking must be brought back to first principles. Rule No. 1 is that *risk models used by banks for their own trading advantage should not double up as supervisory tools.* That, unfortunately, means that the foundation on which Basel 2 and Basel 3 are based, allowing the use of approved internal models by so-called 'sophisticated' banks to set their own capital charges, must be scrapped. True, it also means that risk measures will be cruder, but they will be standardised and applied to all banks. Provided the banks meet those crude standard measures, such as a leverage ratio and broad-brush common risk weightings, they can still use their internal models for trading advantage.

3. 'De-game' risk weights ...

The concept of risk-weighted assets (RWAs) is superficially beguiling. Some assets are surely more risky than others. If regulatory capital ratios are too crude, then there is a danger that banks will 'game' them and put on riskier assets in loopholes not caught by these ratios. This is indeed a risk which needs to be monitored by supervisors and all

---

3 rules) to clear standard over-the-counter (OTC) derivatives contracts on exchanges. According to market reports, hedge funds and other 'shadow banks' are taking some of this business from the big banks active in derivatives. FT 12.09.13: http://link.ft.com/r/6NPSBB/7ZUJ20/5CFRRF/877KIO/B4CL2W/MQ/t?a1=2013&a2=9&a3=12

stakeholders in the bank. *But the principle of allowing banks to set their own risk weightings for regulatory purposes must go.*

4. Put a cap on absolute size ...

It is probably true that absolute size alone does not determine how manageable a bank is. On the other hand, a landscape of giant banks makes management extraordinarily difficult. Moreover, it tends to stifle competition and to tilt the balance between practitioners, regulators and politicians. And, of course, it is not clear that economies of scale get better for banks with assets beyond $100 billion.[12]

In my opinion, *splitting existing global banks into three standalone entities* (retail; corporate/wholesale; investment banking) will go some way to reduce each unit's balance sheet, but more reduction may be needed.

12 See http://www.bankofengland.co.uk/publications/Documents/speeches/2012/speech615.pdf

5. Reduce interconnectedness ...

We mustn't give up on this. There are ways to limit interconnectedness between banks, and between banks and non-banks. We need to use them.

The interbank lending market has already shrunk since 2007 because of more sensitivity about banks' and national banking sectors' creditworthiness, and more recently because of the scandal involving manipulation of Libor, the most common interbank lending benchmark. A financial transaction tax, which makes repo transactions (lending or sale and buyback of securities) more expensive, would further reduce interconnectedness. But regulated banks' exposure as prime brokers and lenders of leveraged loans to hedge funds and private-equity firms is the key. It would be a thing of the past, if they were flatly forbidden to deal with them in that way. Systemic risk arising from interconnectedness would then be confined to the community of investment banks, hedge funds, private-equity firms and sophisticated investors which deal with each other.[13]

6. Put the credit derivatives toothpaste back in the tube ...

Given the damage wrought over the past twenty years by the misunderstanding and misuse of credit derivatives, a rethink is necessary.

One big problem with credit derivatives is that they offer banks and investors a means of getting credit exposure without having to study or research the underlying credit risk. Since one of a bank's core functions is the handling of credit, this is a lazy way of taking exposure – or of protecting

---

13 Some war-gaming is required to test what the contagion risks might be from the failure of one or more shadow banks.

the balance sheet. It is taking us away from a world in which banks have first-hand experience of the companies and other borrowers they do business with. Attempts have been made to restrict the purchase of credit default swaps (CDS) to those who have exposure to the underlying credit risk. It might be difficult for regulators to prevent the bilateral writing of CDSs, but regulated banks and insurance companies could conceivably be forbidden to write them and/or trade them.

7. Encourage new banks …

Creation of new banks in all three categories (retail, wholesale/commercial and investment/shadow) should be encouraged, and barriers to entry lowered across the board. In the retail sector, this would mean encouragement of anything from 'narrow' banks to mutual banks, co-operative banks, communal savings banks, credit unions, standard high-street banks, and person-to-person lending operations such as Zopa. Most retail banks, and Zopa too, tend to rely on a credit bureau to help them decide on credit terms for each borrower. As these credit bureau scores proliferate, person-to-person lending and lending by credit unions may grow more commonplace, offering more competition to incumbent retail banks.

In particular, I would like to see more wholesale/commercial banks in the UK. This would be a new class of bank for us: it would have no retail deposit base, yet it would make both corporate and wholesale loans. Its business model would be similar to that of a German Landesbank, but without the Landesbank's historical flaws.[14] It would fund

---

14 Most German Landesbanken, even those that survived the recent crisis, have a poor reputation after years of poor risk management and delusions of grandeur. One exception might be Hessische Landesbank (though that may be because of its robust risk-management pact, Verbund, with regional savings banks). But there is no obvious

itself in the securities markets and by taking deposits from corporates and retail banks (but not from retail customers).

The work of these banks could possibly be complemented and supported (for instance with partial guarantees) by a development bank along the lines of Germany's state-owned Kreditanstalt für Wiederaufbau (KfW). The Business Bank being set up by the UK government, with around £4 billion of capital to finance small and medium-size firms, is designed to help them find their way through the plethora of government assistance schemes. But it needs to be far bigger to play this role effectively.

It should also be possible to simplify the operation of corporate/wholesale banks. Their core function is to finance companies, municipalities, governments (and perhaps other banks), to offer them a range of other financial services such as foreign-exchange and interest-rate products, and to facilitate such things as bond and share issues. As commercial

reason why a corporate/wholesale bank should be as badly run as the Landesbanken were. It would be designed to serve its client base, not to pile extra risks on its balance sheet because of over-cheap funding.

banks, not investment banks, they would not lead-manage such issues, but they might underwrite part of a bond or share issue for a short time. It is not their business to trade in and out of bonds, shares, derivatives, or other financial instruments for their own account, or even to make markets for clients.

The closest the commercial/wholesale banks might get to conventional investment banking would be lead-managing the financing of a giant project, such as a nuclear power station. There, they would spread the credit risk with other corporate/wholesale banks or engage the services of an investment bank to find non-bank lenders such as investment funds or infrastructure funds. Each bank would be limited to lending only a portion of its overall capital to a single borrower, or to a business sector, such as commercial property, shipping, the automotive industry, etc.

8. Leave the shadow banks alone ...

Investment banking partnerships will have the freedom to work closely with the rest of the shadow-banking sector, in which I include hedge funds, private-equity firms and other alternative investment managers. The only restriction on their activity will be that their financing must not come from regulated retail or corporate/wholesale banks. Instead, they will need to finance themselves by the issue of bonds and commercial paper (of which corporate/wholesale banks may hold only a limited amount), and by tapping hedge funds and other investment funds directly for private placements of debt, equity or subordinated debt and project-specific investments.

Regulators will need to look only at the aggregate numbers, for macro-prudential reasons. If, for example, the commercial property market seemed in danger of overheating, regulators might caution the corporate/wholesale banks and discourage their further lending to the sector. But they would not directly intervene in the activities of the alternative investors.

In my new world, anyone would be able to start his own investment bank – just as anyone can start his own hedge fund. The aim would be to keep this sector as unregulated as possible. However, as a counterparty/clearing member of a stock exchange or other exchange, an investment bank would have to meet the capital and liquidity requirements set by the exchange, as well as its 'fit and proper person' requirements. Otherwise, the investment bank's ability to use leverage will depend only on its relationship with its sources of funding (which will not be regulated banks).

9. Offer a light touch to hedge funds, pension funds and other institutional investors ...

There should be no need to regulate hedge funds or their managers for anything other than fraud, provided (a) that they are not dealing with vulnerable clients, such as financially illiterate or unsophisticated investors; and (b) that they are not getting finance or borrowing securities from a regulated retail or corporate/wholesale bank, or from a regulated pension or insurance fund.

In my new banking world, regulated pension or insurance funds would not be able to invest directly more than a small proportion (say 5% to 10% of their assets) in funds run by hedge fund managers or unregulated shadow banks. In other words, hedge funds, private equity funds and other shadow banks (and the new-style investment banks) would be starved of the kind of cheap leverage they have had in the past. They would then need to draw their capital and leverage either from each other, or from sophisticated private investors. The investment sector is likely to divide itself into those vehicles that have dealings with regulated entities and those that do not.

10. At least *consider* a financial transactions tax ...

It is no surprise that financial actors in general and the City of London in particular are against the imposition of an EU-wide financial transactions tax. The basic idea behind an FTT is to 'throw sand in the wheels of capitalism' – although it has also been promoted as a 'Robin Hood' tax to take some of the turn made by wheeler-dealers and distribute it among the less well-off. Inevitably, therefore, it is an emotional subject.

In my opinion, however, the *principle* of discouraging apparently 'empty' trading (i.e. those trades between financial intermediaries with no end-user in sight, which are themselves often cancelled before execution) is not a bad one.

Would an FTT do *real* damage? I am sceptical. Some experts have objected that it would kill the repo market. Since there are about $16 trillion of repos outstanding at any one time in the American and European markets (according to rough calculations by the New York Fed and ICMA[15]), this would seem to be a real problem. It might well make it uneconomical to trade repos of less than one-year maturity – which would severely reduce the securities activities of shadow banks.[16] But it is not clear to me that they or their investors would suffer as a result.

15 See: http://libertystreeteconomics.newyorkfed.org/2012/06/mapping-and-sizing-the-us-repo-market.html#.U7mTlfldXXs. See also: http://www.icmagroup.org/Regulatory-Policy-and-Market-Practice/short-term-markets/Repo-Markets/repo/

16 See: http://www.icmagroup.org/Regulatory-Policy-and-Market-Practice/short-term-markets/Repo-Markets/icma-european-repo-market-reports-and-white-papers/the-impact-of-the-financial-transaction-tax-on-the-european-repo-market/

3

THE CHANGING FACE OF BANKING CAREERS

The biggest challenge facing employees (and their bosses) in the banking sector that I envisage is how they and their successors will live with much lower expectations: lower pay, less excitement, and, most important, less chance of hitting the jackpot and never having to work again.

Some may choose to move to the pure investment banking and alternative investment sector. But there they will have to live with risk of losses as well as gains. In my opinion, that will be healthier. Many who worked in finance in heady times during the past two decades knew they were being overpaid – but could hardly refuse the money thrown at them. Others may genuinely have believed they were adding value. But most of the value was going to them and their own institution, rather than to the clients they were supposed to be serving.

In the brave new world of sensible financial regulation that I am advocating, *this will change*. Instead, there will be more room for people who genuinely want to serve the real economy. There will also be more room for honest entrepreneurs who are willing (indeed, keen) to operate in an environment that puts them at risk of loss as well as gain.

4

SORTING OUT BRITAIN

In any rethink about the future of the financial system and the financial sector, *Britain is a special case* – not least because the financial sector has come to dominate the British economy and to crowd out other (arguably more useful) economic activity.

I acknowledge that several attempts have been made since 2008 to change the nature of Britain's big incumbent banks and the prevailing culture. These attempts have signally failed. In particular, UK Financial Investments (UKFI), which, as the major shareholder, had the opportunity to make its mark on RBS and Lloyds Banking Group, failed to precipitate change in either the structure of these banks or their management culture. In my opinion, *stronger medicine is needed*.

What should that medicine include? It seems to me that there are three steps to be taken:

1. Nationalisation

In my opinion, RBS and (possibly) Lloyds Banking Group, two of Britain's four biggest banks, should be fully nationalised. This may seem a drastic step, and it is. But it is the only lever the government has to send a clear message that the prevailing culture must change.[17]

In the five years since the rescue of RBS and Lloyds, successive UK governments have failed to make a dent in the way these banks are run or in the way that rewards are shared out. More radical measures are necessary – perhaps with existing private shareholders being offered non-voting preference shares in an equity-for-debt swap. Other 'limping' institutions, such as Nationwide and the Co-op Bank, might also be nationalised. This would give the government a free hand to appoint the management it wants, and to determine remuneration practices throughout these institutions.

Who would run these nationalised banks? They would certainly have to be exceptional people, prepared to take home a fraction of their predecessors' pay, yet able to preside over the conversion of a behemoth into smaller autonomous units. They might be seconded from accounting or consulting firms – but only on the understanding that they will be paid by the bank, not the seconding firm. I am confident such people exist – and that they would come forward.

True, the EU's Competition Commissioner might object that nationalisation amounts to state aid and demand that the banks be returned to the private sector as soon as possible. (However the Directorate-General for Competition says it is agnostic on whether a concern

---

17 I have an unlikely ally in Nigel Lawson, former Chancellor of the Exchequer (1983–88), who wrote of RBS in a Financial Times article in November 2013: "... the government blundered by acquiring only 81 per cent, rather than 100 per cent, of the equity. The existence of the minority shareholding continues to complicate the process of sorting out the RBS mess in the public interest." http://www.ft.com/cms/s/0/7ec12228-453c-11e3-b98b-00144feabdc0.html#axzz2ramEEhJg

is privately- or state-owned, provided the state is not propping it up commercially.) But Britain could point to many examples of state ownership in other EU countries to which the EU turns a blind eye.

2. Breaking up the big banks

For Britain's four or five biggest banks, I believe that there must be a clear split of investment banking from commercial banking (not just a separation of proprietary

trading and prime brokerage for hedge funds, as recommended by Liikanen[18]), and a ring-fencing of retail banking from both commercial and investment banking (as recommended by Vickers[19]). The cleanest solution, in my opinion, would be a separation of each big bank –

---

18 See http://ec.europa.eu/internal_market/bank/docs/high-level_expert_group/report_en.pdf report by the High Level Expert Group on reforming the structure of the EU banking sector, October 2012

19 See https://hmt-sanctions.s3.amazonaws.com/ICB%20final%20report/ICB%2520Final%2520Report%5B1%5D.pdf Independent Commission on Banking, final report, September 2011

RBS, Lloyds, HSBC and Barclays (and perhaps Standard Chartered and Santander) – into three stand-alone entities: retail, commercial/wholesale, and investment banks.

Obviously, the retail and commercial/wholesale banks must be very strongly capitalised. Only then can any 'spare' capital be assigned to the investment bank. But that is not enough. As soon as possible, the ownership of the investment bank must be restructured into a partnership – via a management buyout or a sale to private-equity investors – so that its business is self-financing and its failure cannot affect the retail and commercial/wholesale banking units.[20]

3. Scrapping the bonus pool and capping remuneration

This is tricky, but, in the end, I believe that there is no alternative to a remuneration cap. It is my belief that remuneration of employees at the retail and commercial/wholesale banks should be capped at an inflation-adjusted £200,000. This means that all existing bonus provisions must be suspended and, if there is to be a new bonus system it must be implemented according to completely new guidelines.

The problem is that, despite the lessons of the banking crisis, the concept of the bonus pool lives on. It may not be so generous, and more of the bonus may be deferred or paid in shares, and it may be subject to 'clawback' in later years – but the bonus still plays a big part in negotiations and performance assessments every year. It influences employees' behaviour, and their attitude to

---

20 There is a question whether the separated corporate/wholesale and investment banks can continue to trade under, say, the Barclays name, or whether there must be a distinction at least to the extent that JPMorgan & Co. was split in the 1930s into today's JPMorgan and Morgan Stanley.

senior management, to clients, to each other, and to the bank itself. Seen from outside, it is the curse of modern banking.

For years, bank executives have said they wished they could end this bonus-driven culture. But they have failed to do so for two main reasons: first, it gives them power; and, second, they are scared of losing what they call 'talent'. That is why it needs an initiative from outside. But capping bonuses by itself is not good enough – especially when the cap is not defined in absolute terms, but only in relation to base salary. The remedy has to be to cap total remuneration and to abolish the bonus pool altogether at all banks which have access to the central bank's discount window. That would include all regulated retail and corporate/wholesale banks – but it would not catch investment banks or hedge funds *provided* they are set up as partnerships.

In my new banking world, any EU or third-country banks with subsidiaries in the UK, whose depositors might be protected by UK deposit insurance, must be subject to the same business split and the same remuneration cap as UK banks. I would even argue that EU banks which have 'passported' branches into the UK, should be subject to the same treatment – if this is possible in EU law. And, if it isn't now, *it is something that Britain should demand as part of the renegotiation of its terms of EU membership.*

5

Eight Firm Steps

The main thrust of all these proposals is revolutionary: it is to simplify banks and to change their culture. If Britain is to lead the rest of the developed world in banking reform, these are the steps that any government needs to take:

1. The full nationalisation of RBS and (possibly) Lloyds Banking Group.

2. The breaking up of each of RBS, Lloyds, HSBC and Barclays into three stand-alone entities – a retail bank and a corporate/wholesale bank (each of which should be separately capitalised) and an investment bank (which should be a partnership and must be economically independent of the former parent).

3. The ring-fencing of retail banking at other big banks such as Santander and Standard Chartered.

4. An absolute cap on remuneration at an inflation-adjusted £200,000 and abolition of the bonus pool principle at all regulated banks, i.e. those which have access to the Bank of England's discount window.

5. The prohibition of both market-making and proprietary trading at corporate/wholesale banks in all but standard currency and interest-rate products. For more complex products, such banks may act for clients in an agency capacity only, procuring services from brokers, investment banks, hedge funds or asset managers. And they may take only limited exposure to these counterparties in terms of credit and performance risk.

6. Investment banks must be restructured as partnerships – which would then be free to take risks as they please. Obviously, they would be governed by conduct-of-business rules and by stock-exchange regulation, but there would be no capital requirements. In this sense, they would be indistinguishable from hedge funds – and, indeed, they would trade among themselves, and with hedge funds and other sophisticated counterparties, in a very light regulatory environment.

7. The sale and purchase of credit derivatives by regulated banks would be forbidden – unless they have an offsetting position in the underlying credit.

8. The complex bank capital rules embodied in Basel 2 and 3 would be scrapped in favour of simplified standards for retail and corporate/wholesale banks – such as capital and liquidity ratios based on a percentage of overall assets. Moreover, a similar approach should be encouraged for systemically relevant financial institutions in the US, Germany, France and Switzerland.

PART 2

WHAT WENT WRONG?

6

Mission Creep

Big Bang and the lifting of Glass-Steagall

Banks have always been dangerous, but they became much more dangerous in the 1980s after various steps to liberalise them in America and Britain.

In Britain, after Big Bang in October 1986, banks were allowed to buy and integrate stockbrokers and stockjobbers (the brokers and market-makers in stocks and shares).

In America, the Gramm-Leach-Bliley Act (1999) effectively repealed the Glass-Steagall Act of 1933, which had forced the separation of investment banking from commercial banking activity – for instance, the break-up of JP Morgan & Co. That paved the way for giant 'universal' banks which could use the stability of their retail deposits to take bigger and bigger bets on the wholesale credit, securities and derivatives markets. That turned out to be a recipe for disaster.

Financial engineering: started honest but became self-serving

In their early days, financial derivatives served a real purpose. Trading of interest-rate futures on the Chicago Mercantile Exchange, for instance, and the invention of interest-rate and currency swaps met a genuine customer need. These products offered simpler solutions to complex financial problems. Swaps, for instance, replaced complex back-to-back loans made by pairs of companies in different currencies or different markets. For example, an American company could 'swap' its own fixed-rate debt in dollars for a Japanese company's floating-rate debt in yen. The economic effect would be that they settle the difference in each other's obligations without the extra trouble and expense of raising finance in a foreign currency in which they are not a well-known borrower. Once swaps caught on they greatly widened companies' access to finance in different markets.

However, during the 1990s, the rewards that arrangers could earn for creating more and more complex financial products were simply too tempting. That put a premium on opacity. Perhaps the apogee of this era was creation of the 'quanto' swap – nothing more than a bet on the future difference between short-term and long-term interest rates in a pair of currencies and the exchange-rate risk between them. It had no conceivable economic relevance for the buyer. Libor squared was another – the exchange of cashflows based not on a simple interest rate, Libor, but on its square. Why? For what economic purpose?

Fear of currency and interest-rate volatility and illiquidity

With the explosion in trading, a succession of exchange-rate and interest-rate shocks, and increased globalisation, there was an inevitable tendency towards short-termism and the desire to protect oneself from price volatility. It became increasingly important for financial positions to be tradable. Traders above all wanted financial instruments that were liquid – quickly sellable for cash. And that view affected the behaviour of corporate treasurers and investors. It was a phenomenon that grew exponentially, to the detriment of the underlying economy.

The bloating of the financial sector

As a result of the plethora of new instruments and new financial-engineering techniques, the turnover of the financial services sector naturally grew – as did the share of financial services in UK GDP. This was applauded in Britain by City institutions and by then prime minister Tony Blair and his Chancellor of the Exchequer, Gordon Brown.

The quest for economies of scale

JPMorgan Chase, Barclays and Deutsche Bank now have gross assets of over $2 trillion *each*. However meaningless that number may be, it indicates a huge volume and mix of businesses that is a challenge to manage in good times, let alone at a time of crisis. After all, the assets of Lehman Brothers were 'only' around $640 billion at the time of its collapse in 2008, and the wind-up process is still going on five years later.

And it is not just the balance sheet. Deutsche Bank is not one single entity. It comprises more than 1,000 separate units, including 376 subsidiaries, 394 special-purpose vehicles and 406 significant equity holdings, according to its annual report. In my opinion, there is no 'optimal' size for a bank – but a bank with a balance sheet of $500 billion (or perhaps even $250 billion) is probably too big.

Andy Haldane, executive director of the Bank of England, in a speech on banks' economies of scale in October 2012, made an important, related point. He said that the lower funding costs enjoyed by banks that are 'too-big-to-fail' (i.e. so big that the government would rather rescue them than risk the economic shock of their failure) seem to be the reason why economies of scale at big banks with assets of more than $100 billion continue to improve with size. Take away the advantage of funding that is cheaper because they are too-big-to-fail, he went on, and there is no evidence that bigger banks are more efficient than small ones.[21]

The ascent of credit modelling

As finance became more and more complex, as banks became bigger and as quantitative finance took on a life of its own, financial engineers began to think that credit risk might be just as tradable as interest-rate, currency and equity-index risk had become. They developed models – such as CreditRisk+ and CreditPortfolioView – that aggregated the performance of a portfolio of credits, and applied that aggregate as a proxy for other portfolios. It seemed 'scientific', but it overlooked the fact that credit risk is and always will be very individual. It can only effectively be aggregated in giant portfolios – and then only for certain types of credit, such as consumer debt, mortgages, or car loans, where customer behaviour is broadly consistent and has a long data history.

Unfortunately the financial engineers were more ambitious. They wanted to apply their risk models to company loans, where the big money is. As a result, they invented credit

---

21 See http://www.bankofengland.co.uk/publications/Documents/speeches/2012/ speech615.pdf

default swaps (CDSs). They also developed collateralised debt obligations (CDOs) – bundles of credits which could be sliced and diced to meet a particular investor's alleged appetite for risk. And they convinced the rating agencies to put their stamp of approval on the creditworthiness of each tranche.

Regulators tried to squash this early in the game, but they failed. Banks were soon using their own models of credit risk to reduce the capital charge on credit risks in their portfolios – without being reined in by their regulators.

Regulatory capture

Since 1988, bank regulators have been led a merry dance trying to devise rules that constrain what complex banks are doing. In the process, it is arguable that they have been 'captured' themselves. Banking rulemakers have ended up allowing almost every form of financial innovation – good or

bad. Worst of all, they handed over risk measurement to the banks themselves, allowing them to use their own 'models' to calculate their own regulatory capital requirements.

The Basel Committee on Banking Supervision has over the years produced thicker and thicker volumes on bank capital requirements – which have required bigger and bigger compliance departments to administer. But, ever since the principle was conceded that banks set the pace, supervisors have stumbled to catch up.

The most egregious example of this was the treatment of credit-risk modelling. In September 1998, at a conference sponsored by the Bank of England, various credit-risk models were paraded before regulators, and found wanting. As a result, a decision was taken not to allow credit-risk modelling to mitigate regulatory capital under the pending Basel rules known as Basel 2. That was then.[22]

Within a year or two, with the development of a market in credit default swaps (CDSs), the use of credit-risk modelling had become widespread – and the game was up. The regulators had been finessed, and the notion of offsetting credit risks within a credit portfolio was included (and explicitly recognised) in Basel 2.

Basel 3, which is now being implemented (admittedly sporadically) in various jurisdictions, has taken complexity further – and into new areas. Additional rules for liquidity and the demand for 'living wills' – blue-prints for the orderly wind-up of a bank – have added to the regulatory and compliance burden, not just for banks but for regulators too.

Basel 4, if bank regulators pursue the Basel route, is likely to be even more complex.

---

22 For an account of this meeting see Dealing with Financial Risk, p. 58.

The gaming of risk-weighted assets

Allowing banks to use their own view of risk as a regulatory benchmark is fraught with problems. In particular, highly leveraged investment banks have been able to present a less frightening picture of themselves by using the concept of risk-weighted assets (RWAs). They assign a measure of riskiness to all of their assets using their home-grown models of how risky each asset is – in terms of credit risk, market risk, or any other kind of unpredictability. By this means, Barclays's gross assets of £1,405 billion can be reduced to £157.2 billion (at the end of September 2013). And Deutsche's gross assets of €1,649 billion can be reduced to €355 billion (at the end of December 2013).

Unfortunately, such measures are meaningless without detailed knowledge of how that reduction was made – and that is seldom clear.

However, one thing has become clearer since the crisis: gross assets and their relation to the size of a bank's capital buffer (known as the leverage ratio) are an important indicator. The RWA figure may give some comfort day-to-day, but in times of stress it will not count for much; it is the gross figure on which a bank lives or dies.[23]

As a result, the US Federal Deposit Insurance Corporation (FDIC) fought to retain the use of the leverage ratio while more liberal regulators thought it passé.

Now, the leverage ratio is back in fashion, precisely because it is so hard to game, though recently the ratios to be used under Basel rules, starting in 2017, have been softened.

---

23 Andy Haldane warned against allowing banks discretion in their risk-weighting, in a speech in April 2013. http://www.bankofengland.co.uk/publications/Documents/speeches/2013/speech657.pdf

Superabundance of liquidity

The easy availability of cheap debt, reinforced by banks' ability to securitise assets and get them off the balance sheet (at least in theory), led to a massive expansion of credit from Seattle to Saloniki in the years before the crisis. Low interest rates in the euro zone intensified the effect in countries such as Ireland, Spain and Greece.

In the United States, the combination of easy credit and securitisation amplified a housing bubble which, when it burst (as bubbles usually do), triggered the financial crisis from which we all suffered. With hindsight, a credit bubble in one sector or another, inflated by securitisation, would probably have burst in Europe or America sooner or later anyway. But the fact is that it was the housing bubble in the US which signalled the start of the crisis.

Role of the rating agencies

Whether or not the bursting of the bubble was inevitable, there is plenty of blame to go round.

In particular, many people have pointed the finger at the credit rating agencies. Certainly, the three biggest (Moody's, Standard & Poor's and Fitch) allowed themselves to be drawn into a new and expanding source of income, rating tranches of 'structured' securitised assets, such as CDOs.

This was unknown territory for them, since it involved not only rating the aggregate credit risk of each tranche, but also the quality of the CDO 'manager' who could fine-tune the asset pool by trading the assets. In other words, these were no longer simple corporate credit risks but highly complex animals with a life of their own – a characteristic largely, if not totally, ignored by rating agencies, investors and regulators until it was too late.

Despite the continued difficulty of rating these tranches of securities, the rating agencies are still being asked to provide this service. A rating from one or more of the three agencies is still a requirement for most institutional investments in publicly-traded instruments. And there is a continued conflict of interest, because these rating agencies are usually paid for their services by the issuer of the securities.

Unfortunately, there is no obvious alternative. Other rating agencies have tried to compete, but the experience of Fitch, the youngest of the big three, suggests that it takes years to break into the oligopoly.

Egan Jones, a Pennsylvania-based rater of corporate bonds, has tried to do so – with limited success. So has Jules Kroll, who made his reputation in the spooky world of financial investigation. More recently, Scope, a Berlin-based rater of investment funds, has turned its attention to rating European banks. At least two of these charge investors, rather than issuers, for their services – which takes care of one potential conflict. But it is likely to be years before ratings from any of these agencies are interchangeable with those of the established three.

Arrogance and entitlement
– the new breed of banker

Partners who harness their personal wealth to the fortunes of a financial institution with unlimited liability can, with some justification, pay themselves as much of the proceeds as they think the firm can bear. In the 1970s and 1980s, that is how it was. Wall Street investment banking partnerships would scoop half of the firm's revenues into a bonus pool, from which they would reward themselves and their staff. Some years, they did extraordinarily well; in other years, partners ate losses to keep the show on the road. It was not perfect: bankers still occasionally bet the ranch and lost, but the losses were borne by themselves and their creditors – not the taxpayer.

When those financial institutions changed their status, as most of them did, to joint-stock or publicly-listed companies, they should have changed their remuneration practices. After all, employees and directors may simultaneously be shareholders, but they are not partners: the most they can lose (apart from their job) is their stake in the company. So they are not entitled to treat the firm as their personal pocketbook – as partners did in the past. Unfortunately, the culture of entitlement that characterised the partnership structure survived the change of ownership. Worse, the same culture was picked up by those commercial banks which wanted to break into investment banking. In order to lure top investment bankers, they believed that they had to offer the same kind of deal – or in some cases even more, with bonuses guaranteed for several years.

Bankers increasingly were led to believe that they were masters of the universe, creating value where there was none before. They felt it appropriate to reward themselves out of bonus pools which generally raked off 50% of the revenue (note revenue, not profit) generated by the sale of risky structured-debt products. Since the credit risk involved did not go away, they had unwittingly (or, worse still, wittingly) actually increased the risk of loss for their customers.

Note that there was no question of individual bankers sharing the pain of loss. Their business model allowed them to take a share of the upside, while leaving the downside for others to bear.

Regulators and governments have, from time to time, tried to address this 'agency' problem by ordering the deferral and possible clawback of bonuses over a three- to ten-year period. That may have modified the bankers' sense of entitlement – but it hasn't eliminated it.

This sense of entitlement among financial sector employees is unique. Workers in other sectors, such as retail, healthcare, construction etc, do not demand the same. In the 1980s, investment bankers' pay was roughly equivalent to that of that of other professionals; by 2007, the burgeoning sense of entitlement had meant that it had grown to nearly four times as much.[24]

Moreover the special treatment enjoyed by financial intermediaries has been self-perpetuating. Those who could in theory set limits on banker compensation are often on a similar gravy train: they include employees at institutional shareholders, such as managers of pension funds and insurance companies, corporate executives; compensation consultants; regulators (some of whom might have an eye on a job in the private sector); analysts at banks and rating agencies. None of them have been particularly critical of such levels of compensation – nor have politicians and government officials, who may also be looking at the revolving door.

Moreover, the industry itself and its spin-doctors have been immensely successful in convincing decision-makers that it would be dangerous to interfere with the way they handle remuneration. 'Talent' might flee abroad or into other sectors, leaving finance to be run by the second-rate. Even the most recent efforts to cap bonuses have not attempted or dared to address the entrenched principle of entitlement.

---

24 See Andy Haldane 'reformation speech' (cf. page 13 above). http://www.
bankofengland.co.uk/publications/Documents/speeches/2012/speech616.pdf

Interconnectedness

In the quest to trade higher and higher volumes, financial institutions found ways of shunting liquidity between each other that were almost frictionless. Very little account was taken of the counterparty exposure between the firms. It was like a giant game of pass-the-parcel.

After Lehman Brothers collapsed, the general consensus was that the system could not afford to let other big firms go down. The result was, for example, that the insurance company AIG was bailed out. Why? Because its financial products division was believed to be interconnected with almost all of the other big investment-banking groups. Each one of those groups, and those groups' creditors in turn, would have faced an unknown black hole in its balance sheet if AIG had been allowed to go under. It was widely believed that the developed world's financial system, which was already traumatised, might have ground to a halt.

Maybe that was true. Maybe governments really did have no choice.

The interbank lending market was the first casualty of the trauma. Central banks and then governments had to step in to fill the gap in liquidity provision – allowing banks to post almost any kind of asset with the central bank as collateral for ready cash.

That situation has not changed, even though the crisis has abated. Even today, banks are still refinancing more through central banks than they are with other entities in the market. It may be that the interbank market – in which banks lend to each other short-term without posting collateral – will never reach its former volume. That is probably a good thing. Interbank lending is a convenient way for banks to manage their liquidity, but it has proved highly sensitive to contagion as soon as there is any concern about the creditworthiness of a bank or group of banks. Far better, in my opinion, that banks should find other sources of liquidity – though perhaps not just from central banks.

Despite the demise of the interbank market, banks are still left with huge volumes of bilateral positions with each other, particularly in non-standard swaps and derivatives. Some have been reduced by novation or tear-up, but it is a slow process.

Holding governments to ransom

In the financial crisis of 2008–10, domestic governments in America, Britain, Ireland, Iceland, Germany, France, Italy, Austria, and so on were forced to intervene. In most cases, banks were recapitalised by the governments' purchase of shares in the institutions. Yet only in a very few cases were banks actually nationalised: notably, several Irish and Icelandic banks, and the former British building societies Northern Rock and Bradford & Bingley.

In America, the situation was rather different. Those banks deemed to be 'systemic' were forced to take on $10 billion of government capital, and there was a temporary cap of $500,000 on top executive pay. Moreover, broker-dealers like Goldman Sachs and Morgan Stanley were forced/persuaded to become regulated banks, with access to the Federal Reserve's discount window.

In Britain, the government was more timid. Although two big banks, RBS and Lloyds Banking Group, became

respectively 87% and 43% government-owned, those share holdings (and those in the Northern Rock cluster) were delegated to UK Financial Investments. Although UKFI was an agency within the Treasury, its officials were pretty much ineffective in influencing the banks. Their reticence reflected their belief that the banks should be returned to wider share ownership as soon as possible. The ineffectiveness of UKFI persists today.

Quantitative easing

A mantra during the crisis, endlessly repeated by Ben Bernanke, chairman of the US Federal Reserve, was the need to use aggressive monetary policy to keep the economy from falling into recession/depression. The method used, in both Britain and the US, was quantitative easing (QE), whereby the central bank buys assets with its own money – in theory lowering the price of credit and making credit more accessible to parts of the economy where there is demand.

In its pursuit of QE, the Fed bought a range of assets, including Treasury bonds, agency bonds and agency mortgage-backed securities. That offered direct financial assistance to American non-bank companies. Under Britain's version of QE, the UK Treasury's instruction to the Bank of England allowed it to buy corporate assets as well as gilts (UK treasury bonds). In practice, however, the Bank concentrated almost entirely on buying gilts, which had the effect of pumping cheap finance into the financial system, but not the real economy. The Bank of England purchased only a small volume of corporate bonds and hardly any commercial paper, which means that British QE had little direct effect on non-financial companies.

The big unknown is whether QE, and the resulting very

low interest rates, have done much more than push investments into stock markets, in the search for higher returns, and drive up the price of equities. And the conundrum for the Fed and the Bank of England remains: How does one get the country off the drug of QE without sending the domestic economy (and, in the case of the dollar, emerging markets as well) into a tail-spin?

The euro-zone crisis as destroyer of government/bank symbiosis

Once euro-zone governments had rescued their banks (and apparently stabilised the financial system), creditors began to turn their fire on to the governments standing behind those banks. If the banks' capital consisted mainly of their home nation's government bonds, then, inevitably, they could be no more secure than the governments standing behind them.

In time, it became clear that there could be no real return of confidence unless the euro-zone banks were seen as stable according to a common trans-euro-zone benchmark. The idea of a banking union was born – with the goal of a common supervisor (single supervisory mechanism – SSM – under the European Central Bank), a single resolution mechanism (SRM), and a single rulebook.

But the conundrum remains: To prevent a total collapse of confidence in the banks of some euro-zone countries, their portfolios of home-country government bonds continue to be counted as risk-free, i.e. having a zero weighting among their risk-weighted assets. This is the case even in the latest version of the Basel rulebook, implemented in the EU as CRD 4, at least for banks which do not (or choose not to) use internal risk models to set regulatory capital.

This fudge may be necessary in the short term. After all, where else would governments place their unwanted bonds than with their own banks – which can then post them as collateral for cash with the European System of Central Banks?

But it remains to be seen how long a Europe-wide banking system can live with such a fudge.[25]

---

25 Thomas Mayer, formerly chief economist for Deutsche Bank, has suggested a next step for the euro zone. He argues that the European Central Bank (ECB) should, over time, buy up all the supposedly 'risk-free' government paper held by euro-zone banks at the ECB, and exchange it for genuinely risk-free ECB bonds backed by the joint and several guarantee of all euro-zone member states. A virtue of this proposal is that it would permit the ECB to fine-tune credit growth by adjusting the spread between the cost of central bank reserves and the rate it pays on deposits. On paper, this could work. But it would require the purchase of large volumes of euro-zone government debt by the ECB – which is still a political taboo. http://www.ceps.be/book/copernican-turn-banking-union-urgently-needed

7

HALF-HEARTED FIXES

During the past four years many of the weaknesses in the post-crisis banking and financial system have been addressed. However, it is far from clear that these reforms have created, or will ever create, a financial system that is both safer and a better servant of the real economy.

Various high-level commissions have produced recommendations on how the banking and financial sector might be restructured – notably the Independent Commission on Banking (known as the Vickers Commission[26]) in Britain, and the High-Level Expert Group on reforming the structure of the EU banking sector (known as the Liikanen Report[27]). These have resulted in draft bank reform legislation in Britain, Germany and France and a new framework proposed by the European Commission in January 2014. But a lot of the sharpness of the original recommendations has been lost. Likewise in the United States, the Dodd-Frank Act of

---

26 See https://hmt-sanctions.s3.amazonaws.com/ICB%20final%20report/ICB%2520Final%2520Report%5B1%5D.pdf

27 Liikanen report: http://ec.europa.eu/internal_market/bank/docs/high-level_expert_group/report_en.pdf

2010 has lost its edge in the course of implementation – particularly in the interpretation of the so-called Volcker Rule outlawing proprietary trading at banks.

It is worth reviewing what is going on, and where – if only to explode the notion that the authorities have everything under control, and that we have no need to worry any more about the safety and soundness of the global financial system.

UK bank reform bill

Let's start with the UK. The current UK legislation, which is wending its way through Parliament, does include some of the Vickers reforms – in particular, it requires the ring-fencing of a bank's retail operations, without forcing a complete legal separation. Small banks (i.e. those with core deposits below £25 billion) are, however, exempt from ring-fencing.[28] And certain customers – large organisations and sophisticated private investors – may make deposits with the non-ringfenced part of the bank.

As it stands, the ring-fenced entities will apparently be able to deal with:

- simple derivatives (up to a threshold amount)
- securitisation of their own assets
- debt-equity swaps
- certain 'ancillary' activities

That's quite a big loophole, though they will be prohibited from having exposures to:

- other banks (except for other ring-fenced banks)
- investment firms (except those not authorised to deal in investments as principal or as agent)

---

28 See https://www.gov.uk/government/uploads/system/uploads/attachment_data/file/223566/PU1488_Banking_reform_consultation_-_online-1.pdf

- insurers (including reinsurers and insurance holding companies)
- investment funds and fund management firms
- securitisation companies
- financial holding companies

Another loophole is that they will be allowed to take trade-finance exposures to foreign banks. And they will be able to hedge themselves against default risk that they own. In other words, even ring-fenced banks are going to be doing some pretty fancy stuff; it is not just meat-and-potato 'narrow' banking.

The impact assessment attached to the legislation makes the bold prediction that the Banking Reform Act will produce a net benefit to the UK economy (because of added stability and the reduced severity of a future crisis) of £114 billion over the next 30 years – bravo! However, excuse me if I don't get too excited.

Other initiatives are unlikely to have much impact. In June 2013, for instance, the UK Parliamentary Commission on Banking Standards (chaired by Andrew Tyrie MP) made its own contribution – a barrage of conflicting recommendations in a report called *Changing Banking for Good*.[29]

Among them was a break-up of RBS into regional and business units – although the Commission also suggested a split into a 'good' bank (or banks) and a 'bad' bank (which would remain in government ownership). These suggestions are useful, but, in my opinion, they have confused preserving value for the taxpayer with preserving value for remaining shareholders. We need to take a more radical approach.

29 See http://www.publications.parliament.uk/pa/jt201314/jtselect/jtpcbs/27/2704.htm

Raising banking standards

Of course, the industry is not exactly thrilled at the prospect of radical reform – though it generally concedes that something must be done. Its approach is incremental – and essentially voluntary. In September 2013, Britain's five biggest banks announced that they would fund an independent banking standards body – a body which is emphatically intended not to be just another bank lobby group. This was in response to calls by the Commission on Banking Standards for a 'unified professional body' to be set up, without subsidy, to establish higher standards in the sector. "The body must never allow itself to become a cosy sinecure for retired bank chairmen and City grandees," cautioned the parliamentary report.[30]

The body may help to make bankers more aware of their duties towards their customers, but the likelihood that it will prompt radical change in UK banking is quite small.

---

30 See https://hmt-sanctions.s3.amazonaws.com/ICB%20final%20report/
ICB%2520Final%2520Report%5B1%5D.pdf

8

THE BROADER CONTEXT

The UK is less and less autonomous when it comes to financial regulation – though that may change if and when the government renegotiates its relationship with Brussels (even that will not affect the myriad obligations it has incurred through other multilateral arrangements). It is, therefore, important to understand what is going on elsewhere – and how that impacts on the UK.

Germany: does it need a national champion?

First, let's look at Germany ... Are there lessons we could learn? There is certainly one. It is worth noting that, compared with Barclays (total assets £1.5 trillion), Deutsche Bank (total assets €1.5 trillion) is actually more leveraged. At the end of December 2013, its leverage ratio was 3.1%, compared with Barclays's which was 2.5% at the end of September 2013.

Both banks are also under threat of some kind of segmentation – Barclays from Britain's banking reform bill, and Deutsche from Germany's own bill on de-risking financial institutions. But that's where the similarities end. It is most unlikely that Germany will break up its 'national champion' completely. The Deutsche Bank group will continue to exist, most likely as nominally independent units under a holding company.

That said, Commerzbank, Deutsche's nearest private rival, is shrinking into a more manageable, but less profitable, institution. Commerzbank is also an example of what can happen to a bank which sheds riskier businesses and a lot of

investment bankers, and concentrates on its core customers. It becomes boring, less likely to make extraordinary profits, and a disappointment for its less enlightened shareholders. In my opinion, the answer to that conundrum is not to abandon reform. It is for the bank to find shareholders who have lower expectations. If that doesn't work, it should be taken over by the state, which, in the case of Commerzbank, still owns 17%.

Germany's network of smaller banks (similar to that in Austria) – made up of savings banks and mutual banks – could be a model for other countries to follow. These banks are of manageable size, have regional expertise, and have a simple business model. Their culture is not one of excessive rewards. The greatest danger they suffer from is local political interference – while the second greatest is being hoodwinked into bad investment decisions because of their lack of financial sophistication. Arguably, they may be too small and undiversified to serve the biggest companies (as proponents of the universal banking model assert), but they are able to procure services for them from bigger wholesale and commercial banks, such as the state-owned Landesbanken and the co-operative central bank, DZ Bank. True, both the Landesbanken and the DZ/WGZ Bank group ran into problems some time ago, because of a combination of political influence, delusions of grandeur and bad risk management. But that doesn't disqualify the model itself. Now that some Landesbanken have disappeared through merger or closure, there are realistic hopes that the rest will be better managed; but the danger of political manipulation requires constant vigilance.

Germany's draft banking law, reflecting the Liikanen report, and harmonised with France's draft law, envisages the transfer of trading and market-making activity, above a certain volume, to a separately capitalised entity.[31] That entity would then be permitted to take proprietary positions and to deal with hedge funds, while the commercial bank would lend to companies and to retail customers.[32]

Like Liikanen, the German draft seems to allow the two entities to be owned by the same holding company – provided there is no cross-funding or double counting of capital. However, there is an unresolved issue (just as there is with the Volcker Rule in the US) about what constitutes market-making and where that overlaps with, or runs over into, proprietary trading. There is also a provision, which will be difficult to make stick, that managers who endanger the bank through reckless behaviour can face criminal prosecution and a spell in jail.

Legal experts have pointed out that there are huge difficulties with this. First, if the executive has behaved fraudulently – for instance, by allowing the bank to continue trading while insolvent, or by misleading shareholders in other ways – then prosecution for fraud would be simpler than prosecution under a banking law. Second, it would be extremely difficult to establish that a bad trading decision was 'reckless', except through hindsight. The executive could contend that, given the information he (or she) had at the time, it was a reasonable decision. The danger is that every trading decision that goes bad might become the subject of a lawsuit.

An analysis of the last banking crisis suggests that many

31 German draft (English summary): http://www.bafin.de/SharedDocs/Veroeffentlichungen/ EN/Fachartikel/2013/fa_bj_2013_07_trennbankengesetz_en.html French draft: : http:// www.economie.gouv.fr/files/projet-loi-reforme-bancaire.pdf

32 Liikanen report: http://ec.europa.eu/internal_market/bank/docs/high-level_expert_ group/report_en.pdf

bankers may have traded recklessly. But, to a large extent, they were encouraged to do so by failures of supervision and regulation. They made over-optimistic assumptions about liquidity and the buoyancy of the market – but so did their regulators. Both bankers and regulators should have learned something from this lesson. So if bad bankers deserve to be jailed in future, so do bad regulators.

The EU reforms beyond Liikanen

At the end of January 2014, the European Commission published a proposal for a regulation, based on consultations after the Liikanen report, to "improve the resilience of EU credit institutions".[33] The nub of it is a ban on proprietary trading in credit institutions of above a certain size. Any such trading would have to be done in a legally and economically separate entity.

But the proposal leaves room for many exceptions. Mutual, co-operative and savings institutions might be exempted at the discretion of the national 'competent authority', the proposal says. In fact the competent authority does not automatically have to enforce separation but is allowed to "exercise judgment, using a set of harmonised metrics".

The proposal attempts to harmonise some of the national legislation already in train. But in doing so it looks as though it will allow the universal banking model to survive almost unscathed – provided the competent authority can put up a decent argument. The proprietary-trading ban is due to come into force in January 2017, with full separation of trading entities to be completed by July 2018.

---

33 EU proposal: http://eur-lex.europa.eu/legal-content/EN/TXT/PDF/?uri=CELEX:52014PC0 043&from=EN

The euro zone and the forfeiture of sovereignty

Inevitably, European banks that fall under CRD 4 and other pending EU legislation have their own peculiar systemic problems. Two stand out:

1. The proposed Banking Union, which means that they will no longer be creatures of their home government.

2. CRD 4, which, at the standardised level applied to all but the most sophisticated banks, counts home-government bonds on bank balance sheets as zero-risk weighted. Recently this has been stretching credibility to the limit as far as Greek, Portuguese, even Spanish and Italian, banks and their holdings of national government bonds are concerned.

In my opinion, this is the point at which the euro-zone crisis – and all the anomalies that it has thrown up – has a direct bearing on global bank reform. If euro-zone government debt ever became 'mutual' (i.e. jointly and severally guaranteed) it might be possible to sustain the convention applied outside the euro-zone: that government debt of a bank's domicile, in its home currency, is zero-risk weighted. If there continues to be wide divergence in euro-zone sovereign ratings, then bonds issued by individual euro-zone countries must, at some point, cease to qualify as risk-free assets for their home banks. That will continue to put euro-zone banks at a disadvantage compared with banks of 'normal' countries, whose governments have sovereign control of monetary policy.[34]

As I see it there are four possible outcomes:

---

34 Although the jitters over US T-bills during the budgetary crisis in October 2013 suggest that there are doubts about the risk-free quality of even US Treasury debt.

1. Euro-zone regulators will continue to regard these bonds as risk-free – which is what current EU bank regulation does.

2. They will apply a 'haircut' to liquidity reserves which include government bonds that trade at a discount.

3. They will require banks in countries whose government bonds trade at a discount to replace them with more highly-rated bonds in their liquidity reserve.

4. Euro-zone banks opt for another kind of liquidity buffer, built from another kind of asset. Central bank money has been suggested.

Inevitably, the proposed Banking Union is having a rough passage. Even the European Commission's own legal department sees a potential infringement of sovereignty in a joint resolution fund. But it is not the only piece of EU legislation that is having a difficult time. There is, for instance, also a legal challenge to the planned financial transaction tax (FTT) on the grounds that it should not be applied by stealth in the 17 EU countries that do not support the idea. As for the proposed cap on bankers' bonuses, at a maximum of 200% of base salary, this is meaningless. Fixed salaries are likely to rise to meet supply and demand (there is already evidence of this happening), and banks will have been robbed of flexibility in pay structures.

Switzerland

What can we learn from the beleaguered Swiss? FINMA, the Swiss financial watchdog, has attempted to rein in its two big systemically relevant banks, UBS and Credit Suisse, by demanding extra capital and liquidity under the Swiss parliament's 'too-big-to-fail' legislation.[35] In response, the two banks have gone very different routes: UBS has severely reduced its investment-banking exposures and is concentrating on wealth management, while Credit Suisse is still competing with other global investment banks. The consequent difference in the two banks' risk-weighted assets is dramatic: in investment banking, Credit Suisse now has more than double the amount of exposure as UBS. In private banking and wealth management, however, their risk profiles are roughly the same, and their leverage ratios (according to stringent Swiss criteria) were 4.2% for UBS and 4.5% for Credit Suisse at the end of September 2013.

The United States of America

The US is not exactly a shining light – indeed, in at least one important way, it is heading in precisely the wrong direction.

America's banking assets are not as disproportionately large in relation to GDP as those, for example, in Britain, The Netherlands, Switzerland or even Germany. But, since the crisis, the biggest US banks have been growing, not shrinking. And that is not making them any easier to manage or regulate. Even without the embarrassing example of the 'London Whale' (a $6 billion loss due to misguided internal 'hedging'), JPMorgan Chase has clearly become an unwieldy conglomerate of franchises that not even the talented Jamie Dimon, its chairman and chief executive, can stay on top of. There is no good reason why it should not be split up.

The Dodd-Frank Act (2010) and its Volcker Rule (limiting proprietary trading at deposit-taking banks, and their investment in hedge funds) is designed to force big banks to shrink their riskier businesses or get out of them

---

35 See http://www.admin.ch/opc/de/official-compilation/2012/811.pdf

altogether. But there is quite a gap between rule-making and implementation. Banks such as JPMorgan Chase have a breathing-space until at least July 2015 to comply with the Volcker Rule. Legal challenges could help them extend that deadline for another two years, until 2017. Given the lobbying power of the big banks, further watering down is to be expected.

Proprietary trading versus market-making

What is the difference between proprietary trading (taking risk positions speculatively for the bank's own account), and market-making (taking risk positions in anticipation of filling customer orders)?

In the US, the Volcker Rule (which is part of the Dodd-Frank financial sector reform act) specifies that deposit-taking banks may not carry out proprietary trading, but that they may do market-making. Similarly, the proposed German and French banking reform laws, and the European Commission's latest proposal on bank resilience, allow deposit-taking banks to do market-making up to a certain threshold, but no proprietary trading.

The problem is how to make a distinction between the two. In both cases, banks take positions. Deciding what the intention was behind taking a particular position is no easier than playing poker. A glance at the complex criteria proposed by the four US regulators for applying the Volcker Rule suggests it will not be easy to police.[36]

The EU proposal for a regulation to improve the resilience of credit institutions defines proprietary trading and market-making as follows:

---

36 See http://www.sec.gov/rules/final/2013/bhca-1.pdf and http://www.sec.gov/rules/proposed/2011/34-65545.pdf

'Proprietary trading' means using own capital or borrowed money to take positions in any type of transaction to purchase, sell or otherwise acquire or dispose of any financial instrument or commodities for the sole purpose of making a profit for own account, and without any connection to actual or anticipated client activity or for the purpose of hedging the entity's risk as result of actual or anticipated client activity, through the use of desks, units, divisions or individual traders specifically dedicated to such position taking and profit making, including through dedicated web-based proprietary trading platforms.

'Market making' means a financial institution's commitment to provide market liquidity on a regular and on-going basis, by posting two-way quotes with regard to a certain financial instrument, or as part of its usual business, by fulfilling orders initiated by clients or in response to clients' requests to trade, but in both cases without being exposed to material market risk.

There is no better example of how well-intentioned regulators have got themselves, and the financial world, into a muddle by trying to accommodate existing practices, however opaque. A clear line in the sand would be better.

ENDNOTE

The motive behind these recommendations has been my growing unease, over the past fifteen years, with the way that 'sophisticated' finance has developed into a self-serving, self-congratulating culture – voting itself rewards that are too high and, by implication, cannibalising other parts of the economy.

This is not a rant against millionaires and others who have made and enjoy their own wealth. Nor against those who by some fluke of regulation found that the rules worked in their favour and made them rich. But I am against those who believe, or who anyway maintain, that such flukes have added to the sum of human achievement and the general good. That includes apologists for the current state of affairs in banking and bank regulation.

In Britain, and also in other developed countries, we have seen banking systems evolve that are simply not efficient enough at serving the rest of the economy – and that impose a huge cost on the taxpayer when (as inevitably seems to happen) things go wrong. Attempts at reform have all too often been thwarted by the incumbents. And why not? In their place, I would probably do all I could to preserve my privileges – and the rent that I could extract as a result of them.

To me, that is all the more reason for a powerful force for change to come – from left or right field – and precipitate revolution. I am not a communist, an anarchist or a hopeless romantic – but I am a revolutionary. This would not be a revolution against capitalism, but it would be a revolution in favour of the more efficient use of capital and in favour of a fairer distribution of the real costs and benefits of financial services.

PART 3

GLOSSARY

GLOSSARY

Agency bonds – bonds sold by US government-backed agencies whose debts are guaranteed by the US government.

Agency problem – the temptation that those employed to run a company will put their interests ahead of those of the owners or customers.

Asset-backed securities – securities (see Securities) which are linked to the value of an underlying asset, such as a portfolio of car loans, or credit-card receivables, or mortgages.

Asset pool – a selection of stocks, bonds loans or other financial assets assembled to form the basis of asset-backed securities (see Asset-backed securities).

Back-to-back loan – precursor of the swap (see Swap), whereby two borrowers agree to swap the proceeds of the loans and payments attached to loans raised in different currencies or different markets.

Bad bank – when a bank is rescued or restructured, the unwanted and poorly performing assets are put in a 'bad' bank to be run off or otherwise disposed of. The assets and businesses designated as worth keeping and developing are put in a 'good' bank (see Good bank).

Bail-out – rescue of a failing bank, usually with government money.

Banking union – proposed centralisation of ultimate responsibility for bank oversight in the European Union (EU). The European Central Bank would supervise 130 or so of the banks in the euro area seen as systemic (see Systemic).

Basel Committee on Banking Supervision – an international committee of bank supervisors, originally from 10, now 28, major countries, which meets regularly to develop recommendations on bank supervision. Those recommendations have led to an increasingly complex series of rules, starting with Basel 1 in 1988, then Basel 2 in 1998 and Basel 3, which is being phased in from 2013 to 2019.

Basel 3 – the latest in a series of recommendations on bank capital requirements by the Basel Committee on Banking Supervision (see Basel Committee).

Benchmark – a mutually agreed rate or value for an item that is regularly traded – such as the interbank lending rate (see Libor and Interbank).

Big Bang – a landmark in 1986 when banks in Britain were for the first time allowed to buy brokers (see Broker) and jobbers (see Jobber) that dealt in stocks and bonds. British universal banking was born (see Universal bank).

Bonus – extra pay to an employee, which is related to his performance or that of his department or the entire institution (often an automatic component of bankers' pay).

Bonus cap – an upper limit on bonuses as proposed by some governments after European Union legislation due to come into force in January 2015. It foresees a cap of 100% of base salary, or 200% if shareholders vote in favour at the bank's annual general meeting.

Bonus pool – a share of bank revenues set aside as a source for paying bonuses.

Borrowing securities – borrowing stocks and shares with a view to returning them at the end of the borrowing period. This is usually done in the expectation that the price will fall: the borrower sells the securities he has borrowed, hoping to buy them back in the market at a lower price (see also Short position).

Broker – a facilitator of financial or other transactions between two counterparties.

Broker-dealer – an institution licensed by the US Securities & Exchange Commission to buy and sell securities and offer them to the public.

Capital charge – the amount of a bank's own funds (capital, contingent capital and reserves) which a bank is expected by regulators to hold as a buffer against sudden credit or market shocks.

Cash management – handling the cash needs of a company or institution.

CDO, CLO – see Collateralised debt obligation, and Collateralised loan obligation.

CDO manager – an individual or a firm entrusted with buying and selling assets in the pool designed to back a CDO issue (see Collateralised debt obligation) to maintain performance – for instance by selling loans that might go bad.

Central bank money – money created by a central bank

simply by adding it as a balance-sheet item: the safest money there is, provided the country to which the central bank belongs does not go bust. Central bank money has been created recently to provide quantitative easing to stimulate flagging economies (see Quantitative easing).

Chicago Mercantile Exchange (CME) – a commodities and futures exchange in Chicago. The first in the world to list financial futures, starting with foreign currency contracts in seven currencies in 1972.

Clawback – cancelling all or part of a bonus already awarded if the recipient's or the company's performance turns out poorer than expected.

Clearing member – a trading member of an exchange which also handles trades on behalf of clients, guaranteeing that the client will fulfil its trading commitment.

Collateral – an asset pledged by a borrower to a creditor as a source of value in case he fails to perform on a contract.

Collateralised debt obligation (CDO) – a security whose repayment is supported by an assortment of loans or bonds to different companies. The starting value of the asset pool is designed to be greater than the value of the security, so that the excess value in the loans or bonds can be used as collateral if some of the loans go bad. For example 110 car loans totalling $1,100,000 dollars are resold as securities (1,000 pieces of paper each with a face value of $1,000), whose repayment depends on the performance of all those loans. This means that even if a few of the loans go bad the holder of the security still has a chance of making a profit.

Collateralised loan obligation (CLO) – used to describe a CDO (see CDO) if the debt is comprised of loans.

Commercial banking – taking deposits and providing loans and simple financial services to big and small commercial clients.

Commercial paper – short-term bonds sold by companies, repayable usually in one to six months.

Compensation – a euphemism for pay (see also Remuneration).

Compliance – a part of the banking function which ensures that employees and procedures stick to the rules. Modern banks have a compliance department and compliance officers.

Conglomerate – a collection of associated companies under the umbrella of one brand, or holding company (see Holding company).

Contagion – the effect on other financial institutions or markets if one of them falters.

Contingent capital – capital that is not common equity but a type of loan which converts into equity if the bank is in financial difficulty.

CoCos (Contingent capital convertible securities) – Bonds issued by banks which can be converted into equity if the bank's financial health falls below a specified trigger point.

Co-operative bank – a bank owned by all its members (see also Mutual bank). An exception is Britain's Co-operative Bank which now has a majority of private shareholders since its rescue in 2013.

Corporate assets – bonds or loans repayable by companies.

Counterparty – person or entity on the other side of a transaction.

CRD 4 – The European Union's Capital Requirements Directive 4. The latest in a series of EU bank regulations setting the amount of capital that banks should have relative to the risks on their balance sheet. These directives (CRDs 1–4) closely follow recommendations by the Basel Committee on Banking Supervision (see Basel Committee). CRD 4 is roughly equivalent to Basel 3 (see Basel 3).

Credit bureau – a data company which tracks consumer borrowers' individual credit performance and provides potential lenders with a rough personal credit score.

Credit default swap (CDS) – a form of insurance against the event of a company defaulting on its debt. If there is a default event the insurer pays out and takes over the impaired debt. For example, an investor owning bonds issued by GlaxoSmithKline, buys a CDS which will pay the value of those bonds in full if GSK defaults. In the event of a default the insurer (i.e. the provider of the CDS) pays the investor in full then seeks to recover any residual value in the GSK bonds.

Credit derivative – a generic term for any derivative whose price depends on estimates of whether or not a credit, or bundle of credits, will be repaid in full.

Credit rating agency – an outfit which grades securities issued by companies and other entities according to the probability that they will go into default. The best known are Standard & Poor's, Moody's Investors Service, and Fitch Ratings.

Credit union – a club created to encourage personal savings and to lend those funds to local individuals and small businesses.

Cross-funding – the use of funds raised by one part of a financial group to finance another part of the same group.

Currency swap – a swap agreement (see Swap) based on the difference in cashflows between repayments of debt in two different currencies.

Default risk – the risk that a borrower will fail to make timely payments on a debt.

Deferral – delaying payment of a bonus for a year or more to encourage longer-term behaviour.

Deposit insurance – a scheme that guarantees bank depositors that their deposits (usually to a specified upper limit, such as €100,000) are safe, even if the bank fails.

Derivative – a financial product that derives its price from the variation in price of specified traded items, such as bonds, shares, or interest and currency rates.

Development bank – a bank, usually government-sponsored, which provides finance, usually medium-term loans, for projects and companies in sectors where the government(s) would like to encourage development.

Discount window – a facility offered by a central bank to authorised banks to ensure they have access to liquidity (see Liquidity). It allows banks to raise short-term cash by pledging assets, usually government bonds, but also company shares and loans acceptable to the central bank. A discount is applied so that the borrower receives less cash than the full market value of the assets pledged.

Dividend – a portion of company profits that is paid to shareholders, subject to approval at the shareholders' annual general meeting.

Dodd-Frank Act (2010) – an act passed in the US in the aftermath of the financial crisis encompassing sweeping reforms of bank supervision and weaknesses in the mortgage market.

Downside – the likely loss or other disadvantage that a deal might bring (see also Upside).

Equity-for-debt swap – whereby shares in a company are swapped for bonds. Debt-for-equity swaps are more common, as a way of giving bondholders in a distressed company a chance of gain if the company recovers.

European System of Central Banks – a network formed by all national central banks in the euro zone, with the European Central Bank (ECB) at its centre. The national central banks act as agents of the ECB – i.e., since European monetary union in 1999 they have no longer acted as sovereign and independent central banks.

Euro zone – the group of countries which have the euro as their official currency.

Exposure – level of risk being run in a transaction or group of transactions, in a particular market, or with a particular counterparty (see Counterparty) or sector.

Federal Deposit Insurance Corporation (FDIC) – a US corporation which ensures that bank depositors with deposits up to $250,000 will be repaid in full. It is one of four major US regulators of banking groups, the others being the Federal Reserve, the Securities & Exchange Commission, and the Office of the Comptroller of the Currency.

Filling customer orders – selling customers the assets they have asked for.

Financial engineering – using financial skills to achieve often complex goals, such as matching a company's borrowing needs to its projected cashflows.

Financial transaction tax – a tax applied to financial transactions either as a way to put a brake on trading volumes, or to bring in government revenue.

Fit-and-proper person – someone regarded by the licensing authority as having sufficient integrity and competence to run a regulated financial institution.

Flow monster – nickname given to a global investment bank which trades such large volumes of bonds, shares and derivatives that it stands to benefit from economies of scale and timely information about trends in the market.

Frictionless – used to describe trading that incurs zero or minimal transaction costs.

Front-run – buy assets in anticipation that a client order will drive up the market price, then sell to the client or the market for a quick profit.

Gaming – outsmarting rules in a way not intended by the rulemaker.

Global investment bank – one of a handful of banks which provide investment-banking services in all the world's main money centres.

Good bank – assets and businesses designated as worth keeping and developing when a bank is rescued or restructured. Unwanted and poorly performing assets, not needed in the 'good' bank, are put in a 'bad' bank to be run off or otherwise disposed of (see Bad bank).

Gramm–Leach–Bliley Act 1999 – US legislation which finally allowed commercial banks to deal freely in securities and undertake other investment-banking activities.

Guarantee – a promise to step in for the full amount of a contract if it is not honoured.

Haircut – the discount applied when assets are taken as collateral (see Collateral), to ensure that the market value of the assets comfortably exceeds that of the cash advanced.

Hedge – a financial position taken to reduce a perceived financial risk, such as a currency or interest-rate risk.

Hedge fund – a fund for professional investors which uses various financial techniques, including hedging unwanted risks (hence the name 'hedge fund'), to aim for higher than average market returns.

Highly rated – given a good credit rating by a rating agency (see Rating agency).

Holding company – a company at the top of a hierarchy which owns stakes in other companies seen as part of the group, which is sometimes known as a conglomerate (see Conglomerate).

Housing bubble – a period during which house prices seem to be rising unstoppably, encouraging people to buy houses by borrowing beyond their means.

Infrastructure fund – an investment fund established to fund infrastructure projects, such as building roads, dams and power stations.

Institutional investor – a general term applied to a body which invests funds professionally, such as an insurance company, pension fund or other fund management company.

Instrument – almost any item devised to have financial value.

Interbank – refers to high-volume transactions between banks.

Interconnectedness – in finance this refers to the huge number of bilateral arrangements running between banks active in money, lending, currency and derivative markets. The failure of a single bank can lead to multiple disruptions of these arrangements and possibly the failure of other banks.

Interest-rate swap – a swap agreement (see Swap) based on two interest-rate flows, most usually between fixed-rate and floating-rate interest payments.

Internal model – a model (see Model) used for internal purposes by a bank to calculate the risk of the various assets on its balance sheet. Regulators under Basel 2 and Basel 3 rules (see Basel 3) allow sophisticated banks to use their internal models to calculate regulatory capital charges.

Investment banking – banking that facilitates the issuing and trading of shares and bonds and the financing and financial restructuring of companies.

Issuer of securities – a company or other entity in whose name debt or equity securities are sold to raise money.

Jobber – until 1986, a short-term buyer and seller of securities to and from other dealers in the UK securities markets.

Landesbank – a regional German bank whose main job is to offer wholesale services to local savings banks and their customers. Many Landesbanken stepped outside this narrow brief in the 1980s in an attempt to rival global banks, with dire consequences. They are now trying to get back to their roots and prove that the basic model works.

Lead-manage – to be the bank chiefly responsible for organising an issue of shares, bonds or a syndicated loan (see Syndicated loan) for a company or other entity.

Lehman Brothers – an American investment bank which was allowed to fail in September 2008 – an event seen as a defining moment in the 2008/2009 financial crisis.

Leverage – the amount of assets or liabilities relative to the amount of capital held by a company or financial institution.

Leveraged loan – a loan that is many times larger than the capital base of the borrower. Leveraged loans are often used for acquisitions in which the buyer expects a rapid sale of part of the acquired assets to repay the leveraged loan.

Leverage ratio – the assets of a financial institution divided by its capital – a rough measure of how resilient the institution might be to shocks.

Libor (London Interbank Offered Rate) – an interest-rate benchmark determined by the average rate at which a group of banks in London offer to lend cash to each other short-term (between one and six months).

Libor squared – using the square of the Libor interest-rate as the basis of a swap (see Swap) to amplify the effect of a change in the Libor benchmark (making it more risky and volatile).

Lien – the right to seize and sell an object, such as a house, to recover an unpaid claim on its owner (such as a mortgage).

Liquidity – access to ready cash. Banks must have a reserve of liquidity to meet sudden demands for cash by customers. A market provides liquidity if traders can buy and sell the assets, or other financial instruments quoted, easily, with a narrow difference between the buying and selling price.

Liquidity buffer – a cushion of cash – or assets that can quickly be turned into cash – to protect an institution from financial shocks.

Liquidity reserve – a level of liquidity (see Liquidity) kept by banks to satisfy regulators and the market that they are solvent.

Living will – a published set of procedures whereby the businesses of a still solvent financial institution could be transferred or wound up with minimum damage to the rest of the financial system.

Loan-to-value – the amount lent in a mortgage as a percentage of the estimated value of the property.

London Whale – reference to a fiasco in 2012 when a small London-based department of US investment bank JPMorgan Chase lost an estimated $6.2 billion in trading synthetic credit derivatives.

Macro-prudential – overseeing the safety of the financial system on a big-picture basis.

Management buyout – acquisition of a company by its directors or other employees.

Market-making – being ready, as a trading entity, to buy and sell to customers or other market participants at prices it has quoted in the market.

Master of the Universe – term applied to high-flying investment bankers, or those who think they are.

Maturity – the date, or length of time, by which a loan or bond must be repaid.

Metrics – methods of calculation.

Mitigate regulatory capital – reduce the amount of capital that banks are required by regulators to maintain as a buffer against shocks.

Model – an attempt to formulate complex financial activity in simplified terms, in order to assign probability to different possible outcomes.

Mortgage-backed securities – see Asset-backed securities

Mutual bank – a bank owned by its depositors or members. (See also Co-operative bank).

Narrow bank – a highly conservative banking model, whereby the bank takes deposits and safeguards the funds by investing them purely in risk-free government bonds.

National champion – a company or bank that has global status and is thought to add to national prestige.

Novation – rewriting one or more financial contracts with another party either to provide more clarity or to reduce complexity.

Off balance-sheet – a financial engagement owned or controlled remotely so that its fluctuation in value does not affect the fortunes of the parent institution.

Offsetting credit risk – reducing credit risk for example by buying credit insurance which would compensate for losses if a company loan or bond is in default.

Oligopoly – a market dominated by a handful of big firms.

Partial guarantee – a promise to step in for part of the amount if a contract is not honoured.

Person-to-person lending – lending whereby a private individual takes on the credit risk of loans to one or more persons.

Post collateral – to provide a lender with collateral for a loan or other obligation (see Collateral).

Preference shares – bonds with a coupon that depends on a company's financial performance. Under stress conditions the coupon may not be paid. In a restructuring or bankruptcy, preference shareholders rank higher than holders of common equity, who are the first class of investor to suffer loss, but lower than holders of senior debt.

Prime broker – a provider, usually an investment bank, of financial and other services to hedge funds and private-equity firms.

Private-equity firm – a firm which invests funds, usually gathered from professional investors, in minority or controlling stakes in companies, and which usually has a say in their management.

Private placement – a loan or equity stake placed privately with selected investors rather than through a public offering.

Profit – income generated by trading activity, minus costs.

Proprietary trading – taking speculative trading positions for a financial institution's own account.

Publicly-traded instrument – a financial asset, such as a share, bond or derivative standard enough to be traded on a stock exchange or electronic platform.

Quantitative easing – the use of central bank money to buy assets from the market – usually government bonds – to stimulate a depressed economy.

Quantitative finance – the use of sophisticated mathematics to steer financial trading decisions.

Quanto swap – a currency swap agreement (see Currency swap) in which the interest-rate indexes of the two currencies are switched. For example the yen side is determined by the prevailing dollar interest rate, and the dollar side by the yen rate.

Rating agency – see Credit rating agency

Real economy, the – economic activity that is driven by manufacturing, production or services other than financial services.

Refinance – to raise cash from a bank or central bank by pledging assets, such as shares, bonds or property (see also Collateral).

Remuneration – a euphemism for pay (see also Compensation)

Repo – short for repurchase agreement, which is an agreement to sell securities and buy them back after a certain period. Repos are a cheap way for owners of securities to raise short-term finance (see also Securities lending).

Retail bank – a bank which deals purely with consumers and small businesses.

Revenue – income generated by banking activity.

Ring-fencing – a separation so that a retail bank within a banking group has no financial relationship with other parts of the group.

Risk weight – a percentage grade applied to an asset according to its risk relative to that of a standard loan. For example a bank loan to another bank may be graded as only 20% as risky as a loan to a commercial company; and a loan guaranteed by the state may be graded as having zero risk weight.

Risk-weighted assets (RWAs) – the total of a bank's assets after risk weights have been applied.

Savings bank – a retail bank usually owned by a municipality.

Securities – bonds and shares which are traded on a stock exchanges or electronic platform, or bilaterally.

Securitise – to divide the value of an asset, or bundle of assets, into tradable fragments that are sold to investors.

Shadow bank – entity outside the regulated banking system which nevertheless performs some banking functions, such as making loans and using leverage (see Leverage) to make investments. The broadest definition of shadow bank includes hedge funds, investment managers, and private equity firms.

Short position – an obligation to deliver a commodity or financial asset by a certain date. Often used by dealers who are betting that the price will go down. They create a short position by borrowing or selling, say gold or shares, promising to deliver them at a future date. If the price has indeed gone down they can find them more cheaply in the market and make a profit. If the price goes up they make a loss (see also Borrowing securities).

Short-termism – the inclination to aim financial decisions at short-term results rather than longer-term success.

Single resolution mechanism (SRM) – a procedure which would set up an emergency euro-zone fund intended to help wind up any failing systemic bank (see Systemically significant bank).

Single rulebook – an attempt to draw up a harmonised set of banking rules for the European Union, a task given to the London-based European Banking Authority (EBA).

Single supervisory mechanism (SSM) – a procedure for centralised bank supervision in the euro zone, and other non-euro-zone states which elect to join the SSM.

Sovereign rating – the credit rating of a sovereign country based on the likelihood that it may not make full and timely payments of its debts.

Special purpose vehicle (SPV) – an entity devised to hold specific assets for a financial institution, remotely enough so that failure of those assets, in theory, does not affect the institution.

Spread – the difference between one market price and another, for instance in the buying and selling price of a security.

Standardised model – a method prescribed by bank regulators for calculating the amount of regulatory capital to be held against various classes of risk exposure. Regulators allow more sophisticated banks to use an internal model for the same purpose (see Internal model).

Sticky – refers to bank deposits that, because of customer loyalty or inertia, are unlikely to be withdrawn suddenly, or indeed ever.

Stockbroker – an arranger of trades in shares and bonds and other financial instruments between counterparties (see also Broker).

Stockjobber – an intermediate buyer and seller of stocks and bonds who helps to provide a market with liquidity (see also Jobber).

Structured product – general term for assets or derivatives bundled together by an investment bank for sale to investors.

Subordinated debt – debt that ranks below senior debt in bankruptcy or restructuring proceedings. (See also Preference shares, Contingent capital, and CoCos).

Swap – an agreement to exchange the difference between two sets of cashflows on a notional principal amount (for example $100m), which may be calculated on the basis of different interest or currency rates, or any other type of index.

Syndicated loan – a multi-million loan arranged among a syndicate of lenders, whereby each lends a part of the total.

Systemic – refers to a financial institution big and interconnected enough to affect the financial system and the economy in general if it gets into trouble (see also Interconnectedness).

Systemically relevant bank – see Systemic.

Tax break – favourable tax treatment given by a government to certain kinds of business to encourage their development.

Tear-up – cancellation of one or more contracts with another party to reduce complexity.

Too-big-to-fail – used to describe a financial institution so important to national or international financial stability that its home government would be bound to rescue it if it were threatened with failure.

Trade at a discount – bonds or other type of obligation being valued by the market at less than 100% of their face value, reflecting the risk that they might not be repaid in full.

Trade finance – provision of short-term loans to a company to finance a specific export or import.

Trading exposure – open-ended risk run by institutions engaged in proprietary trading or market-making (see Market-making, Proprietary Trading and Exposure).

Trading risk – ultimately all financial trading can be seen as exchanging one kind of risk for another – hence as the trading of risk.

Tranche – a slice of an investment which is priced or sold separately.

Treasury bonds – bonds issued by the US government.

Underlying credit – the actual determinant of credit performance, (i.e. the actual credit name) used as a reference for a credit derivative.

Underwriting – guaranteeing a minimum price for a new issue of shares and bonds.

Underwriting position – the financial risk involved in underwriting a share or bond issue (see Underwriting).

Universal bank – a bank which provides all types of financial services to a wide spectrum of customers from the man in the street to governments and industrial companies.

Unlimited liability – personal responsibility for all commercial losses of an enterprise.

Upside – the likely profit or other advantage that a deal might bring (see also Downside).

Volcker Rule – a part of the Dodd-Frank Act of 2010 passed in the US in the aftermath of the financial crisis (see Dodd-Frank Act). The Volcker Rule bars big banks from proprietary trading (taking speculative risks for their own account) (see Proprietary trading) or investing their capital in shadow banks (see Shadow banks) such as private equity firms (see Private equity firms) and hedge funds (see Hedge funds)

War-gaming – enaction by participants of a simulated crisis or other scenario to gain some less costly experience of the real thing.

Wind-up process – procedure for closing down a financial institution aimed at causing the least possible mess (see also Living will).

Write – to be the risk-bearer in an insurance or option contract. A writer of a credit default swap (see Credit default swap) bears the risk that the credit in question will default.

Zero risk weight – see Risk weight.

INDEX